LEADING FROM ANY SEAT

The Hard Truths About Trust, Communication, and
Leadership Without Authority

Sandra Miles, PhD

Copyright

Publication Information
Published by DSM Publishing
An imprint of DSM Initiatives, LLC
St. Augustine, FL
ISBN: 979-8-9955531-0-6

DSM PUBLISHING

Dedication

For my mother,
whose strength, grace, and quiet influence shaped how I understand leadership.

For my father,
whose example shaped how I lead.

Table of Contents

Introduction

Why I Started Thinking Differently About Leadership

Why I Started Thinking Differently About Leadership

For many years, I held senior leadership roles where my responsibilities included making decisions, guiding strategy, and overseeing the work of large teams. Like many leaders, I spent much of my professional life thinking about leadership—what it required, how to practice it well, and how to help others develop it.

Then I moved into a new organization where I entered as essentially unranked staff.

For the first time in years, I no longer held formal authority.

At first, I viewed this shift as a break from leadership. Without a title or positional authority, I assumed my role was simply to contribute where asked and support the direction set by others.

In other words, I approached the role the way many people understand followership: as being a good soldier and doing what you are told.

But over time, something became clear.

Even without a leadership title, there was still an expectation that I would exercise leadership.

I was expected to think critically, contribute ideas, influence outcomes, and help move work forward—not because of my position, but because of my experience and judgment.

Initially, this frustrated me.

It felt like I was being asked to act like a leader without being positioned as one.

Only later did I realize that this was exactly the point.

Leadership had never actually disappeared. The title had.

What remained was influence.

What I began to realize is that followership is not the opposite of leadership—it is one of the ways leadership is practiced.

That realization forced me to reconsider how I understood followership. Instead of seeing it as passive support, I began to recognize it as something far more active: leadership practiced without formal authority.

Once my definition of followership expanded, something else expanded with it.

My reach.

A Less Comfortable Realization

At the same time, another realization began to surface—one that was less comfortable.

While I had been viewing my own followership as a form of subservience—selfless and supportive—I also began to recognize how often I had expected that same version of subservience from others when I held leadership authority.

If I did not see a particular type of leadership behavior in someone—regardless of their title—I sometimes interpreted their actions as resistance rather than influence expressed differently.

This realization led me to an important question:

How often are people in organizations receiving two conflicting expectations at the same time?

Some leaders and peers may expect subservience from those without formal authority.

Others may expect those same individuals to exercise leadership from their roles.

Both expectations can exist simultaneously, often without being clearly articulated.

The result is two quiet but significant problems.

First, individuals who attempt to exercise influence from the middle of the organization may receive mixed signals. Some leaders encourage them to lead from their roles, while others push back and expect silent support.

Second, the population of people labeled "followers" is far too large in most organizations for their role to remain this unclear.

In virtually every workplace, the majority of people operate without final decision authority. Yet expectations for how those individuals should contribute, challenge ideas, and support leadership decisions are rarely defined.

When the role of followership remains ambiguous, frustration emerges on all sides.

Leaders may feel unsupported or second-guessed.

Employees may feel constrained, undervalued, or unsure how much influence they are expected to exercise.

Both groups are often responding to the same underlying ambiguity.

Leadership and Followership Are Not Opposites

Part of the confusion stems from how leadership and followership are often framed.

They are frequently presented as opposing roles—one defined by authority and the other by support.

But in most organizations, leadership and followership are not opposites.

They are overlapping responsibilities.

A department head may lead their team while simultaneously following the direction of a vice president.

A vice president may lead a division while supporting the priorities of a president or CEO.

Leadership and followership frequently exist at the same time.

The question, then, is not simply how to lead or how to follow.

The question is how individuals participate responsibly in leadership systems when they are not the final decision-maker.

Leadership Without Formal Authority

Effective organizations depend on more than the quality of decisions made at the top.

They depend on how individuals throughout the organization interpret decisions, communicate concerns, support direction, and contribute to the functioning of the system.

In other words, organizations depend on how people practice leadership when they are not the one in charge.

Followership, at its best, is leadership practiced from a different seat.

This book explores what that form of leadership requires and this concept will discussed in more detail in Chapter 3.

The Leadership Participation Model

Leading From Any Seat

To better understand how individuals contribute to leadership systems without formal authority, this book introduces the Leadership Participation Model: Leading from Any Seat.

The model describes four stages through which individuals and teams strengthen their participation in leadership systems. Each stage builds on the one before it, moving from awareness to collective integration:

Awareness

Recognizing your role in the leadership system—understanding that leadership and followership often coexist.

Interpretation

Responding thoughtfully to situations—challenging assumptions about information, authority, and decisions.

Discipline

Practicing leadership behaviors—exercising judgment, communicating concerns constructively, and supporting direction.

Integration

Strengthening the system collectively—establishing shared norms for how teams lead and follow together.

Each section of this book explores one of these stages.

Part I focuses on awareness, examining why followership is often misunderstood and why its expectations remain unclear.

Part II explores interpretation, challenging common assumptions that shape how people interpret leadership decisions.

Part III focuses on discipline, examining the behaviors that distinguish strong followers from passive participants.

Part IV turns toward integration, providing tools that teams can use to strengthen leadership and followership together.

Participation in the Leadership System

In most organizations, leadership is not confined to a title.

It appears in everyday moments—when someone raises a concern constructively, interprets a situation thoughtfully, supports a decision responsibly, or helps others move the work forward.

These moments often occur far from the final authority in the room.

They happen wherever individuals choose to participate thoughtfully in the leadership system around them.

This book is an invitation to approach those moments differently.

Because effective leadership does not only come from the top.

It also comes from those who understand how to lead from any seat.

Part I – Awareness

Recognizing Your Role in the Leadership System

The Elephant in the Room

Why This Part Matters

Conversations about leadership are common in organizations. Conversations about followership are not.

Most leadership development programs focus on the skills required to guide others, make decisions, and set direction. Yet the majority of professionals spend much of their time operating without final decision authority. They influence outcomes, interpret decisions, and help translate strategy into action. In other words, they are practicing followership.

Despite its importance, followership is often misunderstood. It is frequently associated with compliance, obedience, or passive support. As a result, many professionals struggle to understand what their role requires when they are not the person in charge.

This section explores why followership often feels uncomfortable to discuss and why it is often misinterpreted.

What You Will Learn

The chapters in this section introduce a different way of understanding followership—one that moves beyond the idea of simply supporting leadership.

You will examine why the concept of followership can feel loaded, how expectations of followers are often unclear, and why leadership and followership are not opposing roles but overlapping responsibilities within organizations.

How to Approach This Section

Rather than offering immediate solutions, these chapters focus on reframing how followership is understood.

The goal is to surface assumptions that often go unexamined and to create a shared language for discussing a role that exists across every level of an organization.

Understanding these dynamics provides the foundation for the principles and practices explored in the sections that follow.

Chapter 1

The Hidden Side of High-Performing Teams

The Truth

High-performing teams are not defined only by strong leadership.

They are defined by effective followership—the everyday practices of trust, accountability, and support demonstrated by people who may not hold formal authority.

Why We Resist It

Most organizations invest heavily in leadership development because leadership feels aspirational.

Followership, by contrast, feels uncomfortable.

The word itself can trigger resistance:

- *I'm not a follower—I'm a professional.*

- *I don't want to be seen as passive.*

- *I want influence, not obedience.*

But followership is not about submission.

It is about the reality that in every organization, most people spend the majority of their time leading from within the team, not from the top of the hierarchy.

The healthiest cultures are built by people who understand that supporting leadership is not diminishing—it is stabilizing.

Research That Supports This

This perspective aligns with foundational work in followership and organizational performance:

- Barbara Kellerman argues that followers are not secondary actors, but central drivers of organizational outcomes.
- Ira Chaleff, in *The Courageous Follower*, emphasizes that effective followers provide both support and challenge, strengthening leadership rather than undermining it.

In other words, followership is not the absence of leadership.

It is leadership expressed through responsibility, courage, and contribution.

A Workplace Scenario

Consider two teams with equally talented leaders.

On Team A:

- staff members speak up directly
- decisions are supported once made
- concerns are raised with clarity
- team members take ownership without being asked

On Team B:

- information becomes gossip
- disagreement becomes disengagement
- feedback is expressed indirectly
- execution slows because support is conditional

The difference is not leadership.

The difference is how people show up within it.

High-performing teams are built by people who know how to lead well *and* follow well.

Reflection Prompt

In my current role, do I view followership as:

- a loss of power

  or

- an opportunity to practice leadership through trust and contribution?

Where do I tend to disengage when I am not "in charge"?

Practice: What to Say / What to Do Instead

What Effective Followers Practice

- They support decisions without needing to control them
- They raise concerns early and directly
- They contribute solutions, not just critiques
- They recognize that culture is everyone's responsibility

Language You Can Use

Instead of:

- "Why wasn't I included?"

Try:

- "What is the best way for me to support this direction?"

Instead of:

- "That decision makes no sense."

Try:

-

- "Can I share a concern and offer an alternative perspective?"

Instead of waiting for permission…

Try:

- "Here's what I can take ownership of right now."

The Effective Followership Mindset

I do not need formal authority to practice professionalism, accountability, and leadership.

Chapter 2

Why Followership Feels So Loaded

The Truth

Followership feels emotionally charged because it is often misinterpreted as submission rather than skilled participation in shared leadership.

Why We Resist It

Most professionals do not resist followership because they are unwilling to contribute.

They resist it because the word itself activates something deeper:

- Status sensitivity

  In many workplaces, leadership is equated with value, while followership is equated with lesser importance. Even when unspoken, the hierarchy is felt.

- Fear of invisibility

  People want to know they matter. Being "a follower" can feel like being optional, unheard, or easily overlooked.

- Ego protection

  High performers often build their identity around competence and influence. Followership can feel like being asked to shrink, comply, or defer.

- Historical misuse of power

  Many employees have experienced environments where "just be a team player" was code for silence. In those contexts, followership becomes associated with control, not collaboration.

- Ambiguity of role

  Leadership roles come with formal authority. Followership roles come with expectations — but often no clear language for how to practice them with strength.

So followership becomes psychologically complicated:
People want to contribute, but they do not want to disappear.

Research That Supports This

Research in organizational behavior consistently reinforces that followership is not passive — it is relational and essential.

- Followership theory (Kelley, 1988; Chaleff, 2009) emphasizes that effective followers are engaged, independent thinkers who support mission execution while maintaining accountability and courage.

- Leader–Member Exchange (LMX) theory shows that trust, performance, and team outcomes improve when leadership is understood as a relationship, not a rank. High-functioning teams depend on strong upward partnership, not one-directional authority.

In other words:
Followership is not the absence of leadership — it is one of its most practical expressions.

A Workplace Scenario

A division is undergoing restructuring.
The executive team makes a decision about reporting lines and communicates it in a brief email.
Within hours, frustration spreads:

- "Why weren't we consulted?"
- "They're hiding something."
- "This was handled poorly."

A respected team member says quietly,

"I guess our input doesn't matter anymore."

But what's actually happening is more complex:

The leader made a time-sensitive decision with incomplete information.

The team member is not reacting to the decision itself — but to what it symbolizes:

- loss of control
- fear of being excluded
- uncertainty about value
- distrust of process

The emotional charge is not about followership.

It is about what people believe followership means.

Reflection Prompt

Where in your professional life have you equated being "a follower" with being less important?

Consider:

- Do you feel respected when you are not in the decision loop?
- Do you associate leadership with visibility more than responsibility?
- When do you feel most resistant to being asked to "align"?

Write one sentence:

"Followership feels loaded to me when…"

Practice: What to Say / What to Do Instead

Instead of interpreting followership as dismissal…

Try naming the partnership clearly:

"I may not be in the decision seat, but I can still lead through execution, clarity, and trust-building."

What to Say

When you feel excluded:

"I'd appreciate understanding the context behind this decision so I can support implementation well."

When you disagree without undermining:

"I see the direction. One concern I want to surface early is ___ — not as resistance, but as risk awareness."

When you need voice without entitlement:

"Is there a future point where team input would be helpful, or is this already final?"

What to Do Instead

- Separate participation from control

  You can contribute meaningfully without steering every outcome.

- Assume complexity before assuming secrecy

  Most workplace decisions are constrained, not conspiratorial.

- Practice visible alignment

  Support does not mean silence — it means constructive engagement.

- Redefine followership as execution leadership

  Strong followers create stability, clarity, and momentum — even without authority.

Closing Reframe

Followership feels loaded because most people were never taught how to do it with dignity.

But effective teams do not run on authority alone.

They run on:

- trust
- communication
- shared ownership
- courageous support

Followership is not a lesser role.

It is one of the most underdeveloped leadership competencies in modern organizations.

Chapter 3

Leadership Without Formal Authority

The Truth

Followership is the practice of leadership behaviors — judgment, communication, accountability, and influence — exercised without formal authority.

A Common Leadership Saying

A common leadership saying suggests that people must first learn to be good followers before they can become effective leaders.

There is some truth in that idea. Leadership requires humility, awareness, and the ability to support the work of others.

But the relationship between leadership and followership is often misunderstood.

In most organizations, these roles are not opposites. They are overlapping responsibilities.

A department head may lead their team while simultaneously following the direction of a vice president.

A vice president may lead a division while supporting the priorities of a president or CEO.

Leadership and followership frequently exist at the same time.

For this reason, effective followership requires something deeper than compliance.

It requires individuals to bring a leadership mindset to the role—even when they are not the one making the final decision.

When people approach followership this way, they contribute judgment, perspective, and accountability rather than simply waiting for direction.

In most organizations, individuals move between leading and following depending on the situation. Some may hold formal authority in one context while supporting another leader's direction in a different context. Others may not hold formal authority at all but still carry significant responsibility for the success of the work.

Regardless of title, effective followership requires more than just agreeing to be the good soldier.

Individuals who approach their role without a leadership mindset are more likely to focus narrowly on personal preferences, resist decisions they did not control, or shift responsibility upward when outcomes become difficult. In contrast, individuals who bring a leadership orientation to followership approach their role differently. They consider the broader needs of the organization, the constraints decision-makers may be balancing, and the influence they themselves bring to the system.

Followership, at its best, is leadership practiced from a different seat.

Why We Resist It

Most professionals have been taught to associate leadership with position. Titles signal authority. Authority signals control. Control signals leadership. So when people hear the word *followership*, they instinctively assume the opposite: compliance, passivity, or diminished influence.

But that assumption reveals a deeper misunderstanding about how organizations actually function.

In most workplaces:

- The majority of decisions are executed by people without formal authority.

- Team credibility is shaped by people who do not hold the final vote.

- Organizational momentum is sustained by individuals who influence outcomes from within the system rather than from the top of it.

Still, many professionals resist identifying with followership because doing so can feel like accepting a smaller identity.

Several psychological dynamics contribute to this resistance:

Identity attachment

High performers often build their professional identity around being seen as leaders. Being positioned as a "follower" can feel like a downgrade rather than a role within a larger system.

Control bias

People are more comfortable when they feel they can steer outcomes. When authority sits elsewhere, uncertainty increases.

Cultural messaging about leadership

Books, conferences, and corporate narratives frequently celebrate bold leaders while rarely discussing the disciplined practice of followership.

The result is a paradox.

Organizations need strong followership to execute strategy —

but individuals are rarely taught how to practice it with confidence.

Research That Supports This

Scholarly work on followership consistently challenges the assumption that influence only flows downward.

Robert Kelley's followership model (1992) describes effective followers as individuals who combine independent critical thinking with active engagement.

These followers do not simply comply — they contribute insight, challenge ideas constructively, and take ownership of outcomes.

Similarly, Ira Chaleff's work on courageous followership (2009) emphasizes that followers have a responsibility not only to support leaders but also to question decisions when necessary for the health of the organization.

Leadership scholars increasingly recognize that effective organizations depend on distributed influence, where leadership behaviors occur across multiple roles rather than residing solely at the top of the hierarchy.

In practical terms:

Leadership is a set of practices, not just a role.

Followership is how those practices are exercised without formal authority.

Operating effectively in grey areas requires the same behaviors often associated with strong leadership.

A Workplace Scenario

A senior leader announces a new strategic initiative.

The decision is made. The direction is clear.

Two managers respond very differently.

Manager A

Privately questions the strategy but says little in meetings.

Expresses skepticism informally with peers.

Implements the change slowly, waiting to see if the initiative loses momentum.

Manager B

Raises a few thoughtful questions early to clarify expectations.

Once direction is confirmed, communicates the initiative clearly to their team.

Identifies potential implementation challenges and offers solutions.

Both managers lack the authority to change the strategic decision.

But only one practices leadership through followership.

Manager B does three things that strengthen the organization:

- translates strategy into action
- surfaces operational risks constructively
- reinforces alignment once direction is set

None of those actions require formal authority.

They require ownership of execution.

Reflection Prompt

Think about a time when you supported the implementation of a decision you did not personally make.

Consider:

- Did you view your role as implementing someone else's plan?
- Or did you see yourself as responsible for helping the plan succeed?

Complete this sentence:

"When I practice leadership without formal authority, I…"

Practice: What to Say / What to Do Instead

Shift the Frame

Instead of thinking:

"I'm just executing someone else's decision."

Try:

"My role is to translate direction into results."

What to Say

When clarity is needed:

"To implement this well, it would help to understand the priority behind this decision."

When surfacing operational concerns:

"One implementation challenge I see is ____. Would it be helpful for me to propose a solution?"

When aligning publicly after discussion:

"Now that we have direction, I'll make sure our team understands the goals and timeline."

What to Do Instead

Translate strategy into action

 Strong followers help teams understand what decisions mean in practice.

Surface risks early

 Leadership without authority includes identifying obstacles before they grow.

Reinforce alignment

 Once direction is clear, effective followers help stabilize the team.

Lead through credibility

 People often follow the colleague who demonstrates clarity, calm judgment, and reliability — regardless of title.

Closing Reframe

Leadership is often described as the ability to influence outcomes.
But influence does not require authority.

Every organization depends on individuals who:

- ask thoughtful questions
- clarify direction
- support execution
- hold the work together during uncertainty

These behaviors are not secondary to leadership.
They are leadership — practiced from a different seat.
Followership, at its best, is leadership through influence in the absence of a title.

Part II — Interpretation

Responding thoughtfully to situations

Hard Truths of Leadership at Every Level

Why This Part Matters

What began as a single slide titled *Hard Truths About Effective Followership* in a much broader presentation, has become the foundation for the ideas explored in this section.

Once followership is understood as a form of leadership without formal authority, a different set of expectations begins to emerge.

Effective followership requires more than good intentions. It requires discipline in how individuals interpret information, communicate concerns, and respond to decisions they do not control.

In organizations, many tensions arise not from dramatic leadership failures, but from small misunderstandings in how people interpret situations and respond to them.

These moments often reveal the difference between reactive participation and responsible followership.

What You Will Learn

The chapters in this section explore several "hard truths" that frequently shape workplace dynamics.

You will examine how assumptions about missing information can lead to unnecessary mistrust, why involvement in every decision is neither realistic nor necessary, how indirect communication can create confusion, and why organizations require both transparency and discretion.

You will also explore the importance of recognizing that multiple perspectives may be valid at the same time.

How to Approach This Section

These chapters are intentionally direct.

Each principle challenges common assumptions that often influence how people interpret leadership decisions and organizational behavior.

The goal is not to criticize individuals or leadership structures, but to clarify patterns that appear repeatedly in organizations.

Recognizing these patterns makes it easier to respond thoughtfully rather than reactively.

Chapter 4

Information I Don't Have Is Not the Same as Information That Is Being Hidden from Me

The Truth

Not having information is not the same as information being intentionally withheld.

Why We Resist It

In modern organizations, information is often treated as a proxy for status.

Being included in conversations signals influence. Being excluded from them can feel like a loss of importance.

So when people discover that decisions were discussed somewhere they were not present, the reaction is often immediate:

Why wasn't I told?
Who knew about this before I did?
What else is being kept from us?

The absence of information quickly becomes a story about intent.

Several psychological dynamics contribute to this reaction.

Status sensitivity
People often interpret access to information as a sign of professional standing. When they learn that others were aware of something earlier, the instinctive response is to question whether their role is valued.

The human need for explanation
When information is incomplete, the mind fills the gap. Unfortunately, the story we create is often more dramatic than the reality.

Past experiences with poor transparency

In organizations where communication has historically been inconsistent, employees may become conditioned to assume that information gaps reflect deliberate concealment.

The pace of leadership decisions

Leaders frequently operate under time pressure or with incomplete data. Information may emerge gradually rather than through a single, coordinated disclosure.

What feels like secrecy is often something simpler:

- a conversation that happened earlier,
- a study that needed to be completed before conclusions could be drawn,
- or a decision that was not yet ready for broader discussion.

The problem is not always the absence of information.

The problem is how quickly the absence of information is interpreted as evidence of wrongdoing.

Research That Supports This

Organizational research shows that people naturally construct meaning when information is incomplete.

Sensemaking theory, developed by Karl Weick, explains how individuals interpret uncertain situations by building narratives that help them make sense of what they observe. When facts are missing, people often substitute assumptions.

Research on psychological safety (Amy Edmondson) also highlights the importance of environments where employees feel comfortable asking questions rather than silently forming conclusions. Teams function more effectively when clarification is normalized.

Together, these insights reinforce a simple point:

When information is incomplete, people do not remain neutral. They interpret.

The quality of those interpretations can shape the level of trust inside the organization.

A Workplace Scenario

A leadership team gathers to review the results of a financial analysis commissioned months earlier.

The findings are sobering.

At the institution's current rate of spending, financial projections show that the organization has roughly 42 days of operational runway without continued revenue flow. In practical terms, the institution has almost no financial reserves.

The purpose of the meeting is clear: understand the data and begin discussing possible solutions.

But before the conversation moves toward problem-solving, another question emerges.

One leader speaks up.

> "Shouldn't the entire staff know this? If something happens, that's a lot of people who could suddenly be out of work."

Another leader responds differently.

> "Sharing this widely right now could create unnecessary panic. The people in this room are here because we're responsible for helping solve the problem."

Then a third concern surfaces — and the tone of the meeting shifts.

One participant asks:

> "Why didn't anyone tell us this study was happening in the first place?"

To them, the issue is no longer just financial risk.

It is trust.

If executive leaders knew the situation was serious enough to commission a study, why had others not been informed earlier? Was the lack of communication a lie of omission?

The question triggers immediate defensiveness from some leaders who had commissioned the analysis.

From their perspective, the study had been an attempt to quietly gather accurate information before alarming the organization unnecessarily.

But the conversation has already moved away from the financial challenge.

The focus has shifted to who knew what — and when.

What began as a meeting to address a serious institutional risk ends with a different outcome.

A smaller group is asked to continue participating in the solution-oriented discussions.

Those who treat their presence in the meeting as an opportunity to help solve the problem remain involved.

Those who focus primarily on why they were not included earlier are seen as introducing more tension than progress.

The organization still faces the same financial challenge.

But the meeting reveals something equally important:

When information surfaces late in a process, it is easy for people to interpret the gap as intentional concealment — even when the original intent was caution rather than secrecy.

Reflection Prompt

Think about a time when you believed information was being withheld from you at work.

Ask yourself:

- What information was actually missing?

- What explanation did you assume at the time?

- Did you ever confirm whether that explanation was accurate?

Complete the sentence:

"When I don't have information at work, I tend to assume…"

Practice: What to Say / What to Do Instead

What to Say

Instead of:

"Why wasn't this shared with us?"

Try:

"It seems like there may be context I'm missing. Could you help me understand how this decision developed?"

Instead of:

"This feels like something is being hidden."

Try:

"Understanding the background behind this will help me support the work more effectively."

What to Do Instead

Ask for context before assuming intent
Clarifying questions strengthen trust. Accusations weaken it.

Separate timing from exclusion
Sometimes you were not excluded. The information simply emerged earlier in a smaller group.

Avoid amplifying speculation
Rumors fill information gaps quickly and often become accepted as fact.

Focus on the present opportunity

Being invited into the conversation now may be more valuable than dwelling on why you were not included earlier.

Closing Reframe

Most organizations do not struggle with deliberate secrecy.

They struggle with the challenge of communicating complex information at the right time to the right group of people.

When every information gap is interpreted as intentional concealment, trust erodes even when no deception exists.

Effective followership requires a different discipline:

seeking understanding before assigning motive.

Information you do not have may still exist.

But it is not always being hidden.

Chapter 5

I'm Not Entitled to Be Involved in Every Decision

The Truth

Being responsible for outcomes does not mean being involved in every decision that contributes to them.

Why We Resist It

Most professionals want to contribute meaningfully to their organizations.

That instinct is generally healthy. It reflects engagement, pride in one's work, and a desire to see the organization succeed.

But in many workplaces, the desire to contribute can quietly evolve into something else: the expectation of inclusion in every decision that affects the work.

When people discover that decisions were made without their involvement—or that their preferred option was not chosen—the reaction often feels personal.

Common thoughts surface quickly:

Why wasn't I included?
Don't they trust my judgment?
How can they expect me to support something I didn't agree with?

Underneath these reactions are several powerful dynamics.

Professional identity
High-performing professionals often see themselves as thoughtful contributors. When their perspective is not reflected in the final decision, it can feel like a dismissal of their expertise.

Ownership of outcomes

When individuals feel accountable for results, they may believe participation in every decision is necessary to protect the quality of those results.

Status and influence

Participation in decision-making is often associated with authority. When involvement decreases, people sometimes interpret it as a loss of influence.

But organizations cannot function if every decision requires universal agreement.

In complex systems, decisions occur at many levels simultaneously.

Some require broad input.

Others require speed.

Others must remain within a smaller group because one leader ultimately carries the responsibility for the outcome.

Effective followership requires understanding this distinction:

influence and involvement are not the same thing.

You can contribute meaningfully to an outcome even when you were not present for the decision that produced it.

Research That Supports This

Leadership research consistently highlights the importance of decision clarity within organizations.

Frameworks such as the RAPID decision model emphasize that different roles exist within decision processes: recommending, agreeing, performing, inputting, and deciding. Not every role participates at every stage.

Similarly, research on decision rights shows that clearly defined authority improves both speed and execution. When people understand who is responsible for which decisions, organizations function more efficiently.

When those boundaries are unclear—or when individuals reject them after the fact—friction grows.

The challenge is not always the decision itself.

Often the challenge is how people respond once the decision has been made.

A Workplace Scenario

An organization determined that changes to its leadership structure were necessary to address several internal challenges affecting performance.

Multiple restructuring options were discussed among senior leaders.

Ultimately, the president of the organization made the final decision.

The president's choice, however, was not the option most of the leadership team preferred.

In the week before the decision was formally announced to the organization, something subtle began to happen.

Members of the leadership team began telling colleagues that a major change was coming.

They also made sure to clarify one thing:

"None of the leadership team supported this decision."

The message was repeated in quiet conversations across the organization.

The president, employees were told, had acted alone.

Some leaders went further, explaining why the change would likely be harmful for the company.

By the time the official announcement was made, most employees had already formed an opinion about the decision.

Many received the news with skepticism, anxiety, or outright frustration.

A year later, the results of the restructuring were clear.

The changes addressed many of the operational challenges the organization had been facing. By most objective measures, the business was performing better.

Yet morale across the organization remained unusually low.

The restructuring was still spoken about negatively, and criticism of the president continued.

Interestingly, the leaders who had quietly expressed their disagreement ahead of the announcement remained widely respected. Many employees viewed them as the only leaders who had been honest or protective of the staff.

The organization had successfully implemented a strategic decision.

But the way leaders responded after the decision was made had shaped how the entire organization experienced the change.

The decision itself had not created the distrust.

The response to the decision had.

Reflection Prompt

Think about a time when a decision was made at work that you disagreed with or were not involved in making.

Ask yourself:

- Did my reaction help the organization move forward?

- Did I separate my disagreement from my responsibility to execute?

- How did my words about the decision influence how others perceived it?

Complete the sentence:

"When I disagree with a decision that has already been made, my responsibility as a professional is to…"

Practice: What to Say / What to Do Instead

What to Say

Instead of:

"I didn't support this decision."

Try:

"Now that the direction is clear, our focus should be making the implementation successful."

If clarification is needed:

"Understanding the reasoning behind the decision will help us execute it effectively."

If concerns remain:

"There may be some implementation risks we should monitor as this moves forward."

What to Do Instead

Distinguish disagreement from responsibility
You may disagree with a decision and still play an important role in ensuring its success.

Avoid distancing language
Statements that separate you from the decision can undermine trust across the organization.

Model alignment after the decision
Healthy debate is valuable during decision-making. Once direction is set, alignment becomes essential.

Lead through execution
In many organizations, the credibility of leaders is shaped less by which decisions they preferred and more by how they help the organization move forward afterward.

Closing Reframe

Being excluded from a decision—or seeing a different option chosen—does not automatically signal disrespect.

Organizations rely on individuals who can do two things well:

contribute their perspective during the decision-making process, and support the outcome once a decision is made.

Effective followership requires both.

Leadership without formal authority often means helping the organization succeed even when the final decision was not your own.

Chapter 6

Accusations Disguised as Questions Are Not Helpful

The Truth

Questions that contain hidden accusations rarely create understanding; they often create defensiveness instead.

Why We Resist It

Most professionals want to be thoughtful and respectful in workplace conversations.

As a result, many people avoid stating concerns directly. Instead, they frame their concerns as questions.

Sometimes this comes from a good place. Questions can open dialogue, invite perspectives, and help teams reach better decisions.

But in many organizational conversations, the question is not actually seeking information.

It is expressing criticism.

Examples appear frequently in meetings:

"Did anyone think about how this would affect the team?"
"Was this decision actually discussed with the people doing the work?"
"Did leadership consider the impact this would have?"

These questions are rarely neutral.

They often contain an implied statement:

Someone failed to consider something important.

The problem is that when criticism is delivered indirectly, the conversation becomes harder to navigate.

Several dynamics contribute to this pattern.

Indirect communication feels safer
 Framing a concern as a question can feel less confrontational than stating it directly.

Plausible deniability
If the question creates tension, the speaker can claim they were simply seeking clarification.

Organizational norms around politeness
Many workplaces discourage direct disagreement, leading people to soften criticism rather than express it clearly.

Power dynamics
When employees feel uncomfortable challenging authority openly, they may disguise criticism as curiosity.

Unfortunately, this approach rarely produces the clarity people hope for.

When a question contains an accusation, the listener often responds to the accusation rather than the issue.

The result is a conversation that moves away from the real problem.

Research That Supports This

Research on psychological safety, particularly the work of Amy Edmondson, shows that teams function best when people can express concerns directly and respectfully.

Indirect criticism tends to increase misunderstanding because the actual concern remains unclear.

Communication research also shows that ambiguity in conflict discussions increases defensiveness. When the message is not stated clearly, the listener often interprets the underlying intent rather than the literal words.

In practice, this means that questions containing hidden criticism often escalate tension rather than resolve it.

A Workplace Scenario

During a university leadership meeting, administrators were discussing budget reductions and the possibility of closing several student support offices.

The financial pressures facing the institution were significant, and leaders were working through difficult decisions about how to maintain long-term stability.

At one point in the discussion, someone asked:

"Did anyone even consider the students when these solutions were being put together?"

The question immediately shifted the tone of the room.

Although framed as a question, the statement carried a clear implication: that the leaders responsible for the proposed changes had failed to care about students.

In response, several decision-makers became defensive.

They began explaining how deeply they cared about students and how seriously they took the responsibility of protecting student outcomes.

The conversation quickly moved away from the financial realities facing the institution.

Instead, the discussion turned toward demonstrating support for students, as if fiscal sustainability and student support were competing priorities rather than connected ones.

The original problem—how to address budget pressures responsibly—received less attention as the meeting continued.

In retrospect, a different response might have helped bring the underlying concern into the open.

Instead of responding defensively, someone might have asked:

"What decisions have we made that suggest we don't care about students?"

That question would have surfaced the concern directly and allowed the group to address the actual issue rather than debating motives.

When accusations remain hidden inside questions, conversations often drift away from the real work that needs to be done.

Reflection Prompt

Think about a time when you asked a question at work that carried frustration or criticism.

Ask yourself:

- Was I genuinely seeking information?

- Or was I expressing disagreement indirectly?

-

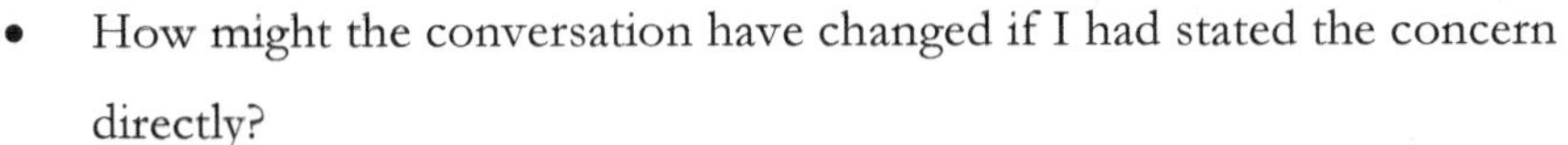

- How might the conversation have changed if I had stated the concern directly?

Complete the sentence:

"When I feel strongly about an issue at work, I sometimes ask questions like…"

Practice: What to Say / What to Do Instead

What to Say

Instead of:

"Did anyone think about how this will affect students?"

Try:

"I'm concerned about how this decision may affect students. Can we discuss that impact?"

Instead of:

"Did leadership consider the consequences of this?"

Try:

"I'd like to raise a concern about the potential consequences of this approach."

Direct concerns create clarity.

Hidden accusations create confusion.

What to Do Instead

State concerns clearly

Direct communication allows teams to address the real issue.

Separate curiosity from criticism

Questions should seek understanding, not deliver judgment.

Invite discussion rather than implying failure

Framing concerns constructively keeps conversations focused on solutions.

Focus on the problem, not the motives

When conversations shift toward defending intentions, progress slows.

Closing Reframe

Questions are powerful tools for learning and collaboration.

But when questions contain hidden accusations, they rarely produce understanding.

They produce defensiveness.

Effective followership requires a simpler discipline:

say the concern you actually mean to raise.

Clarity allows organizations to solve problems.

Indirect criticism rarely does.

Chapter 7

Transparency Inspires Trust at All Levels

The Truth

Transparency is not only about sharing information; it is about ensuring that information travels accurately between levels of an organization.

Why We Resist It

Most professionals say they value transparency.

Leaders want teams to feel informed.
Employees want to understand how decisions are made.

Yet transparency often breaks down in subtle ways.

One of the most common breakdowns occurs when communication consistently flows through a single interpreter rather than directly between the people involved.

This dynamic rarely begins with bad intentions.

Managers and team leaders often believe they are helping by translating information between levels of the organization. They may try to soften difficult messages, advocate for their teams, or simplify complex decisions before passing them along.

But when one person consistently becomes the interpreter between two groups, something important begins to happen.

Narratives start to shift.

Messages become summaries rather than conversations.
Intentions become interpretations.

And over time, trust begins to relocate toward the person controlling the narrative.

Several dynamics reinforce this pattern.

Convenience

It is often easier for leaders and employees to communicate through an intermediary rather than engaging directly.

Relationship loyalty

People tend to trust the individuals they interact with most frequently.

Conflict avoidance

Indirect communication allows difficult conversations to be filtered or softened before reaching the other party.

Perceived advocacy

An intermediary may position themselves as advocating for one group to another, strengthening their credibility with both sides.

None of these motivations are inherently problematic.

The challenge emerges when an organization begins to rely heavily on interpreted communication rather than direct communication.

When this happens consistently, leaders and teams may both believe they understand each other, even when the messages they are receiving have been reshaped along the way.

Transparency does not fail because information is hidden.

It fails because information changes as it travels.

Research That Supports This

As discussed earlier in this book, research on Leader–Member Exchange (LMX) shows that trust and performance improve when communication between leaders and team members is strong and direct.

High-quality relationships between leaders and employees are built through consistent, transparent interaction.

When communication becomes heavily mediated through intermediaries, however, information distortion becomes more likely.

Organizational communication research shows that messages passed through multiple interpreters often change over time. Each retelling introduces emphasis, omission, or interpretation.

This does not always happen intentionally.

But the result is the same: the original message gradually becomes something else.

When leaders and teams rely primarily on interpreted communication, they are no longer responding to the same information.

They are responding to different versions of it.

A Workplace Scenario

In one organization, a senior leader was known for trusting their managers to run their teams independently.

As long as the work was completed successfully, the senior leader rarely interfered with how managers handled day-to-day decisions.

One manager quickly learned how much influence this structure created.

When discussing ideas with their supervisor, the manager often framed their preferences as requests from the team.

"The staff are really asking for this."

In reality, the ideas frequently originated with the manager.

But presenting them as team concerns made approval easier.

When the team agreed with the outcome, the arrangement worked smoothly.

When disagreements emerged, however, the situation became more complicated.

Employees who disagreed with certain decisions assumed the direction had come from senior leadership. The manager quietly reinforced that perception.

"I raised that concern, but the senior leader was firm about it."

Over time, frustration began to grow among team members.

Occasionally, an employee would bring their concerns directly to the senior leader. But these conversations usually happened only after frustration had already built.

From the senior leader's perspective, the employee appeared to raise problems frequently. The manager, meanwhile, was seen as supportive and aligned.

The result was an unfortunate pattern.

The employee began to look like someone who "always had a problem," while the manager appeared to be advocating on their behalf.

Eventually, the employee decided to leave the organization.

Only later did documented information surface showing that several requests attributed to the team had never actually come from them.

The senior leader realized that the narrative they had trusted was not entirely accurate.

The discovery damaged the relationship between the senior leader and the manager.

But the behavior itself was never formally addressed.

By that point, the employee most affected by the situation had already left the organization.

Why This Matters

Situations like this do more than create interpersonal tension.

They can also affect how organizations make decisions and evaluate performance.

When information is consistently filtered through a single intermediary, leaders may unknowingly base decisions on incomplete or inaccurate representations of what teams are experiencing.

Employees, meanwhile, may interpret leadership decisions through explanations that do not fully reflect leadership's intent.

Over time, several risks begin to emerge:

Leaders may respond to concerns that were never widely shared.

Teams may attribute decisions to leaders who were never responsible for them.

Individuals who raise concerns directly may appear difficult rather than insightful.

Perhaps most importantly, organizations may begin making strategic decisions based on narratives that are shaped by interpretation rather than reality.

None of this requires malicious intent.

It only requires a communication structure where messages consistently pass through interpreters.

When this occurs, even well-intentioned leaders can find themselves managing outcomes based on distorted information.

And the people experiencing the consequences may never realize how the distortion occurred.

Reflection Prompt

Think about a time when you relied on someone else to interpret what another level of the organization was thinking.

Ask yourself:

- Did I confirm the information directly with the source?

- Was I hearing a message or someone's interpretation of the message?

- How might the situation have changed if the conversation had happened directly?

Complete the sentence:

"When information travels through several people before reaching me, I tend to…"

Practice: What to Say / What to Do Instead

Encourage direct communication

When possible, create opportunities for conversations to occur between the people directly involved.

Clarify interpretations

If a concern is attributed to someone else, consider asking:

"Would it be helpful for us to discuss this together so we can make sure we're hearing the same concerns?"

Separate messages from interpretations

When relaying information, distinguish between what was said and how it was understood.

Create occasional direct contact across levels

Organizations function best when leaders and teams have periodic opportunities to engage directly rather than relying entirely on intermediaries.

Closing Reframe

Transparency is often described as the willingness to share information openly.

But transparency also depends on something less obvious.

It depends on how accurately information travels through the organization.

When communication flows directly between levels, trust strengthens.

When communication is consistently filtered through interpreters, trust can weaken—often in ways leaders cannot immediately see.

Transparency does not require every conversation to happen publicly.

But it does require that the messages people hear reflect reality rather than interpretation.

Chapter 8

Multiple Things Can Be True at the Same Time

The Truth

In complex organizations, competing perspectives can all contain elements of truth at the same time.

Why We Resist It

Many workplace conflicts begin with a simple assumption:

If one perspective is correct, the other must be wrong.

This type of thinking feels natural. People tend to experience their own perspective as the most complete version of reality because it reflects their responsibilities, pressures, and daily experiences.

When disagreements arise, conversations often become framed as opposing sides.

Leadership versus staff.
Efficiency versus compassion.
Financial responsibility versus mission.
Strategy versus culture.

These oppositions can feel real and urgent.

But in many cases, the tension is not between truth and falsehood.

It is between different responsibilities and different vantage points.

Leaders may be balancing financial realities that others cannot fully see.

Employees may be experiencing operational challenges leaders do not directly feel.

Both perspectives may contain legitimate truths.

The difficulty arises when people assume that acknowledging another perspective means abandoning their own.

When conversations become framed as *either/or*, organizations often become stuck defending positions instead of solving problems.

Effective followership requires a different mindset.

Instead of asking:

"Which side is right?"

A more productive question becomes:

"What truths exist on both sides of this issue?"

Leadership maturity often involves moving from either/or thinking to both/and thinking.

Research That Supports This

Research on sensemaking, particularly the work of Karl Weick, explains how individuals interpret organizational events through the lens of their roles, experiences, and available information.

Different positions within an organization often produce different interpretations of the same situation.

Leadership research also highlights the importance of cognitive complexity, the ability to hold multiple perspectives simultaneously when navigating difficult decisions.

Leaders and teams who develop this capability are better able to manage complexity because they recognize that many organizational tensions involve competing priorities rather than competing truths.

Workplace Dichotomies

Many organizational tensions become easier to understand when people shift from either/or thinking to both/and thinking.

For example:

It is possible that a decision will create tension between groups and still be the best decision available given the circumstances.

It is possible that students may feel disappointed about the loss of a program and that eliminating the program creates financial and physical space for a different program that will ultimately serve students well.

It is possible that frontline staff could be valuable contributors to solving certain problems and that they cannot be included in every stage of discussion when confidential information is involved.

These tensions do not always have simple resolutions.

But recognizing that multiple truths can exist often allows conversations to move forward more productively.

When people acknowledge that different perspectives may each contain valid concerns, discussions shift from defending positions to exploring solutions.

Reflection Prompt

Think about a recent disagreement at work.

Ask yourself:

- What perspective did I believe was correct?

- What perspective did others believe was correct?

- What responsibilities or constraints might have shaped each perspective?

Complete the sentence:

"In this situation, it may be true that…"

Then try identifying two realities that may exist at the same time.

Practice: What to Say / What to Do Instead

Instead of framing disagreements as oppositional, try language that acknowledges complexity.

Instead of:

"Leadership clearly doesn't understand the impact of this decision."

Try:

"Leadership may be balancing factors we cannot fully see, while we are experiencing impacts they may not fully feel."

Instead of:

"This decision is either good or bad."

Try:

"This decision may solve some problems while creating others we will need to manage."

What to Do Instead

Look for competing responsibilities

Different roles within an organization carry different obligations.

Separate intent from impact

A decision can be well-intentioned and still create real challenges.

Avoid binary thinking

Complex organizational problems rarely have simple right-or-wrong answers.

Focus on integration

The goal of organizational dialogue is not to prove one perspective correct but to find ways to address multiple realities.

Closing Reframe

Organizations are complex systems made up of people with different responsibilities, pressures, and perspectives.

When individuals insist that only one perspective can be valid, conversations often stall.

But when teams recognize that multiple truths can exist at the same time, something important happens.

Disagreements become easier to navigate.

Collaboration becomes more possible.

And solutions become more thoughtful than either side might have created alone.

Effective followership requires the maturity to recognize that complex problems rarely belong to a single perspective.

Often, the first step toward progress is acknowledging that more than one truth may exist.

Part III — Discipline

Practicing leadership behaviors

Followers Who Lead

Why This Part Matters

Understanding the dynamics of followership is only the beginning.

The next step is translating those insights into daily behavior.

Strong organizations are not built solely through effective leadership at the top. They are built through the consistent actions of individuals throughout the system who exercise judgment, communicate clearly, and take responsibility for the work around them.

In this sense, followership becomes a daily practice of leadership.

What You Will Learn

The chapters in this section examine the behaviors that distinguish strong followers from passive participants.

You will explore how effective followers exercise independent judgment, communicate concerns constructively, protect the integrity of information, and support decisions once direction has been established.

You will also examine the difference between passive criticism and responsible participation in leadership systems.

How to Approach This Section

Rather than focusing on titles or authority, this section focuses on behavior.

These practices can be exercised by anyone within an organization—whether they lead a department, manage a team, or contribute as an individual professional.

The goal is to help readers recognize how influence operates in everyday interactions and how responsible followership strengthens the leadership systems around them.

Chapter 9

What Strong Followers Practice Daily

The Truth

Effective followership is not passive support. It is the daily practice of leadership behaviors exercised without formal authority.

Why This Matters

Much of the leadership literature focuses on the behaviors of people with authority.

But most organizational outcomes are shaped by individuals who are not the final decision-makers.

They manage projects, guide teams, contribute expertise, and influence how decisions are interpreted and implemented.

In other words, they operate in the space between direction and execution.

When followership is misunderstood as compliance, organizations lose a tremendous amount of leadership capacity.

People wait for instruction rather than exercising judgment.
Concerns remain unspoken or are expressed indirectly.
Decisions are implemented reluctantly rather than responsibly.

In contrast, strong followers actively strengthen the functioning of the organization.

They do not simply respond to leadership.

They help make leadership work.

Over time, several consistent practices distinguish strong followers from passive participants.

Research That Supports This

Research on followership, particularly the work of Robert Kelley and Ira Chaleff, emphasizes that effective followers are not passive or dependent.

They combine independent thinking with active engagement.

Strong followers support organizational goals while also exercising judgment, raising concerns constructively, and contributing to the success of the broader system.

In this sense, effective followership reflects many of the same behaviors associated with strong leadership.

The difference is not the behaviors themselves, but the context in which they are practiced.

What Strong Followers Practice

1. Exercising Independent Judgment

Strong followers do not wait for permission to think.
When given responsibility, they make reasonable decisions within the scope of their role rather than repeatedly seeking approval for every step.

This behavior strengthens trust.

In contrast, followers who constantly ask for clarification or permission—even on routine matters—often create a different dynamic.

Supervisors begin to feel responsible for monitoring small decisions, which can unintentionally reinforce micromanagement.

Over time, what began as uncertainty can become a pattern of unnecessary oversight.

Strong followers help prevent this cycle by demonstrating thoughtful judgment and accountability.

2. Understanding Before Improving

Many professionals join new organizations with valuable experience and strong ideas.

But effective followership requires first understanding the system you have entered.

Consider a common scenario.

A new team member joins an organization with significant experience and immediately begins suggesting improvements based on practices from previous roles.

Each suggestion is met with explanations about existing policies, procedures, or organizational constraints.

The experienced professional may feel that their ideas are being dismissed.

Meanwhile, existing team members may interpret the suggestions as criticism of practices that are shaped by factors outside their control.

Strong followers recognize the importance of learning the organization before attempting to improve it.

They ask questions about the history, constraints, and reasoning behind current approaches.

They observe how decisions are made and how different parts of the organization interact.

Only then do they begin offering suggestions in ways that are informed by context rather than assumption.

Experience is valuable.

But effective followership requires pairing experience with curiosity.

3. Communicating Concerns Directly

Strong followers do not disguise concerns through sarcasm, passive resistance, or indirect commentary.

They communicate clearly and respectfully when something needs attention.

Direct communication allows issues to be addressed early, before frustration grows or misunderstandings deepen.

Indirect communication, by contrast, often creates confusion and defensiveness.

Effective followers understand that raising concerns is part of responsible participation in leadership systems.

How those concerns are expressed matters.

4. Protecting the Integrity of Information

Organizations depend on the accurate flow of information.

Strong followers take this responsibility seriously.

They represent concerns accurately rather than reshaping them for personal advantage.

They avoid exaggerating problems or filtering information in ways that distort reality.

And when sharing information between groups, they distinguish clearly between what was said and how it was interpreted.

This practice helps maintain trust across teams and leadership levels.

5. Supporting Decisions Once They Are Made

Healthy organizations benefit from open discussion during decision-making.

Different perspectives help leaders consider risks, trade-offs, and unintended consequences.

But once a decision is made, strong followers shift their focus from debate to implementation.

They help translate decisions into action and support the team in moving forward.

This does not require suppressing legitimate concerns.

It requires recognizing that effective organizations cannot function if every decision is continually revisited.

Strong followers understand the difference between constructive dialogue and prolonged resistance.

Reflection Prompt

Consider your own role within your organization.

Which of these practices do you demonstrate consistently?

Where might you be relying more on direction than judgment?

And how might your influence increase if you approached your role with a stronger leadership mindset?

Practice: What to Say / What to Do Instead

When clarity is needed:

"Here's how I'm planning to approach this. Let me know if you'd like me to adjust the direction."

When offering improvement ideas:

"Before suggesting changes, I'd like to understand how this process developed."

When raising concerns:

"I see a potential challenge we may want to address early."

When supporting implementation:

"Now that the direction is clear, let's focus on making it work well."

Closing Reframe

Strong followers are not defined by their proximity to authority.

They are defined by how they use their influence.

They exercise judgment.

They communicate clearly.

They strengthen the integrity of the system around them.

In doing so, they practice leadership—not from the top of the organization, but from wherever they sit within it.

Chapter 10

One Bad Apple Spoils the Bunch: When Followership Breaks Down

The Truth

Ineffective followership rarely announces itself openly.

Instead, it appears through behaviors that distort information, avoid responsibility, or quietly undermine the work of the organization.

These behaviors are often dismissed as personality conflicts, workplace drama, or simply "office politics." In reality, they represent a breakdown in how individuals participate in leadership systems.

In most organizations, attention is focused on leadership failures at the top. Yet leadership systems are shaped not only by those with formal authority, but also by how individuals throughout the organization interpret information, communicate concerns, and contribute to decisions.

When participation becomes manipulative, disengaged, or indirect, even strong leadership structures can begin to weaken.

Recognizing ineffective followership is not about assigning blame. It is about understanding the patterns that prevent leadership systems from functioning effectively.

Why We Resist Naming It

Many organizations hesitate to identify ineffective followership directly.

It can feel uncomfortable to acknowledge that individuals without final decision authority still hold meaningful responsibility for how leadership systems function.

As a result, behaviors that distort or undermine organizational progress are often explained away.

Manipulation may be framed as "strategy."

Avoidance may be described as "politics."

Disengagement may be interpreted as frustration rather than withdrawal from responsibility.

In reality, ineffective participation in leadership systems often emerges through these quieter dynamics.

The challenge is not simply poor leadership at the top. It is how individuals throughout the organization choose to participate—or withdraw—from the work of leadership.

Research That Aligns With This

Leadership scholars have long emphasized that leadership systems depend on the quality of participation between leaders and followers.

Research on followership highlights the active role individuals play in shaping organizational outcomes rather than simply responding to direction (Carsten et al., 2010; Uhl-Bien et al., 2014).

Similarly, research on leader–member exchange (LMX) demonstrates that trust, communication, and mutual accountability influence how effectively leaders and followers work together (Graen & Uhl-Bien, 1995).

When individuals distort information, disengage from responsibility, or avoid direct communication, the quality of those relationships deteriorates—and the leadership system becomes less effective as a result.

Workplace Patterns That Undermine Followership

Ineffective followership can appear in many forms, but several patterns emerge repeatedly in organizational life.

Recognizing these patterns helps individuals and teams identify behaviors that weaken leadership systems before they become deeply embedded.

Manipulation and "Alternative Facts"

One of the most damaging forms of ineffective followership involves manipulating information to serve personal goals.

Rather than communicating concerns or perspectives transparently, individuals may reshape information as it moves through the organization.

This may appear as:

- presenting personal preferences as group consensus

- selectively sharing information upward or downward

- framing issues in ways that distort the underlying reality of a situation

In these cases, individuals may maintain influence while avoiding direct accountability for their positions.

Over time, however, the consequences become clear. When information is filtered or manipulated, trust across leadership levels begins to erode.

Leaders lose confidence in the accuracy of what they hear from their teams. Team members become uncertain whether their perspectives are being represented honestly.

Effective followership requires protecting the integrity of information, even when doing so involves raising concerns that may be unpopular.

Poor Leadership Disguised as "Politics"

Organizational politics are often described as inherently negative, but politics themselves are not the problem.

Politics simply reflect the dynamics of influence within a system.

Healthy political behavior can include:

- advocating for ideas

- negotiating competing priorities

- building coalitions to advance important initiatives

These activities are natural in complex organizations.

Problems arise when influence is used primarily to protect individual positions rather than strengthen the organization.

In these situations, ineffective participation is often justified as "just how things work around here."

Decisions may be delayed, conversations redirected, or responsibility avoided in ways that protect individuals while preventing meaningful progress.

When poor leadership behavior is dismissed as politics, the underlying issue remains unaddressed: individuals are prioritizing personal advantage over responsible participation in the leadership system.

Effective followership requires engaging in influence ethically—advocating for ideas while maintaining accountability for the broader organizational outcome.

Quiet Quitting and Quiet Firing

A third pattern involves withdrawal from responsible participation in the organization.

This withdrawal can occur from multiple directions within the leadership system.

Quiet quitting occurs when individuals disengage from the work of the organization while remaining in their role.

Rather than raising concerns directly or contributing to solutions, they limit their participation to the minimum requirements of the job.

This may appear as:

- withholding ideas or effort

- declining to engage in problem solving

- allowing initiatives to struggle without raising concerns early

In some cases, quiet quitting emerges from burnout or frustration with leadership decisions. Those experiences may be real.

Yet within leadership systems, quiet quitting still represents a withdrawal from responsible participation.

Effective followership requires engaging constructively with the work—even when individuals disagree with direction.

A related but distinct dynamic is quiet firing.

Quiet firing occurs when leaders attempt to push individuals out of the organization indirectly rather than addressing concerns openly.

Responsibilities may be reduced, workloads altered in ways that make success increasingly difficult, or expectations shifted without clear explanation.

Over time, the role becomes increasingly frustrating or undesirable, leading the individual to leave voluntarily.

Quiet firing allows leaders to avoid difficult conversations and formal accountability.

However, it also signals to the broader organization that problems are addressed through avoidance rather than transparency.

Both quiet quitting and quiet firing weaken leadership systems because they replace direct communication with withdrawal or indirect pressure.

Effective leadership—and effective followership—require addressing challenges openly rather than allowing disengagement to become the default response.

Workplace Scenario

These patterns rarely appear in isolation. In many organizations, they emerge together as situations unfold - shaping how people interpret events in real time.

A leadership team is discussing a proposed operational change that would require several departments to adjust how their work is organized.

During the meeting, one manager raises a concern about how the change might affect their team's workload. The concern is discussed briefly, and the senior leader facilitating the conversation explains that the issue will be considered as the proposal is refined.

After the meeting, the conversation begins to shift in smaller settings.

One manager tells their team that the decision is "already made" and that senior leadership is ignoring feedback. Another explains to colleagues that several leaders are opposed to the idea but that "politics" are preventing them from speaking openly.

Neither statement is entirely accurate. Concerns were raised in the meeting, but the proposal is still under discussion.

Over time, the narrative that spreads through the organization begins to diverge from the reality of the conversation.

Some employees disengage from the process, assuming that their input will not matter. Others begin framing the issue as a political conflict between leaders rather than a complex decision still being evaluated.

Meanwhile, senior leaders become frustrated by what appears to be growing resistance to a decision that has not yet been finalized.

The problem was not simply disagreement about the proposal. It was how the situation was interpreted and communicated.

It was the way information moved—and changed—as it moved through the leadership system.

Rather than communicating concerns transparently or engaging directly in the decision-making process, individuals reshaped the narrative in ways that protected their own position while distancing themselves from the outcome.

By the time the decision is finalized, the organization is not only addressing the operational challenge that prompted the proposal.

It is also managing the erosion of trust that occurred as the situation unfolded.

Reflection Prompt

Think about a time when a leadership challenge in your organization was shaped not only by a decision itself, but by how individuals participated in the situation.

Were there moments where information may have been filtered or reshaped as it moved through the system?

Did influence operate transparently, or were important conversations redirected or avoided?

Did individuals remain engaged in solving the problem, or did participation gradually withdraw?

Which of these patterns might have been present?

More importantly, how might the situation have evolved differently if individuals involved had approached the moment with a stronger commitment to responsible participation in the leadership system?

Closing Reflection

Ineffective followership rarely appears as open defiance.

More often, it emerges through subtle behaviors—manipulating information, avoiding responsibility, or quietly withdrawing from meaningful participation in the work.

These patterns can exist within any organization and at any level of authority.

Recognizing them is not about assigning blame. It is about understanding how leadership systems break down when participation becomes indirect, disengaged, or self-protective.

When individuals choose transparency over manipulation, accountability over avoidance, and engagement over withdrawal, they strengthen the leadership systems around them.

And in doing so, they help ensure that leadership can function effectively from every seat in the organization.

The question, then, is not simply how to recognize these patterns, but how to respond to them differently when they appear.

Chapter 11

From Passive Criticism to Active Support

The Truth

It is easy to critique decisions from the sidelines. Responsible followership requires something more difficult: contributing to solutions and supporting the work once direction is set.

While the previous chapter examined how followership can break down within organizations, this chapter focuses on how those situations can be interpreted and approached differently in practice.

Why We Resist It

Most professionals have experienced frustration with decisions made by leaders.

They may disagree with the approach, believe another option would have been stronger, or feel that important perspectives were overlooked.

In these moments, criticism can feel justified.

But criticism carries little responsibility.

It is possible to critique a decision endlessly without participating in the work required to move the organization forward.

Passive criticism allows individuals to distance themselves from outcomes. If a decision succeeds, they benefit from the success. If it fails, they can say they disagreed all along.

This posture protects personal credibility, but it does little to strengthen the organization.

Active support, by contrast, requires ownership.

It requires individuals to move beyond commentary and engage with the work of implementation.

For many professionals, that transition—from critic to contributor—is where followership becomes leadership.

Workplace Scenario: Raising Concerns Without Ownership

A leader presents a new initiative to their team and asks them to begin moving forward with implementation.

During the discussion, one team member raises several practical concerns about how the idea might function in practice. The concerns are thoughtful and highlight potential challenges the leader had not fully considered.

After hearing the feedback, the leader decides to pause implementation and revisit the proposal in order to address the concerns raised.

At this point, the team member expresses surprise that their feedback influenced the decision. Their intention had not been to improve the proposal, but simply to ensure that their disagreement had been recorded in case the idea later failed.

This interaction reveals an important distinction.

Raising concerns as a form of protection is different from raising concerns as a contribution.

Effective followership assumes that concerns are raised with the intention of strengthening decisions, not simply creating distance from potential outcomes.

When individuals raise issues constructively, they help leaders see risks they may not have considered.

When concerns are offered primarily to protect personal credibility, the conversation shifts from collaboration to self-preservation.

Healthy leadership systems depend on a different norm.

Concerns are raised to improve decisions.
And once those concerns are heard, the focus shifts toward strengthening the path forward.

Research That Supports This

Research on organizational commitment and psychological ownership suggests that individuals who take responsibility for outcomes—even when they are not the final decision-makers—are more likely to contribute constructively to team performance.

Studies on team effectiveness also highlight the importance of collective accountability, where members of a group support shared decisions even when those decisions were not their preferred option.

In healthy leadership systems, people contribute their perspectives during the decision-making process and then align their efforts toward implementation once a decision has been reached.

This balance between open dialogue and responsible support is essential for organizational progress.

Workplace Scenario

Imagine a leadership team discussing a significant operational change.

During the discussion, several perspectives emerge. Some leaders strongly support the proposal, while others raise concerns.

One member of the team disagrees with the direction but chooses not to share their perspective directly in the meeting. Instead, they remain quiet during the discussion.

Later, when the decision is announced to the broader organization, that same individual privately tells colleagues that the plan is flawed and that leadership did not listen to important input.

The result is predictable.

Confidence in the decision erodes.
Employees become uncertain about the direction.
And the leadership team appears divided.

In contrast, responsible followership would have required a different approach.

Concerns could have been raised clearly during the decision-making process.

Once the decision was made, the responsibility would shift toward supporting implementation rather than undermining the outcome.

Reflection Prompt

Think about a recent decision in your organization that you disagreed with.

How did you respond?

Did you raise your perspective during the decision-making process with the intention of improving the decision, or simply to ensure your disagreement was noted?

Once the direction was set, did your actions support progress—or did they create distance between you and responsibility for the outcome?

In moments like this, effective followership requires more than having the right perspective. It requires contributing to the work of making decisions stronger and supporting the team once a direction has been chosen.

Practice: What to Say / What to Do Instead

When you disagree during discussion:

"I see the potential benefits of this approach, and I also want to raise a concern about how it might affect this area."

When the decision is finalized:

"While this wasn't my preferred direction, I'm committed to helping us make it successful."

When colleagues express frustration:

"The decision has been made. Let's focus on how we can make it work well."

When uncertainty emerges:

"Here's how we can move forward with clarity."

Closing Reframe

Passive criticism is easy.

Active support requires leadership.

Effective followers do not simply evaluate decisions from the sidelines. They participate in the work required to make decisions succeed.

They offer perspective during discussion.

They align their efforts once direction is clear.

And they help the organization move forward—even when the path chosen was not their own.

This is not compliance.

It is leadership practiced from within the team.

Part IV — Integration

Strengthening the system collectively

Field Guide for Every Team

Why This Part Matters

The ideas explored throughout this book are most powerful when they are discussed and applied collectively.

Leadership rarely occurs in isolation. It is shaped through conversations, interpretation, and collaboration among individuals working within the same system.

For this reason, effective followership is not simply an individual practice. It is also a team practice.

What You Will Learn

This section provides tools that leadership teams and organizations can use to apply the principles explored in earlier chapters.

You will encounter real workplace scenarios that illustrate common tensions, discussion prompts designed to encourage honest conversations among teams, and a practical framework for establishing shared norms around followership and leadership behavior.

How to Approach This Section

This section is designed to be interactive.

Readers may choose to reflect individually on the scenarios and prompts, or leadership teams may use them as discussion tools in meetings, retreats, or professional development settings.

The goal is not to produce immediate agreement, but to create space for meaningful conversation about how leadership and followership function within a team.

When these conversations happen openly, organizations are better able to develop the kind of leadership systems that support both effective decision-making and responsible followership.

Chapter 12

Applying the Principles of Effective Followership

The Truth

The principles of effective followership become most visible in everyday workplace situations.

They appear in how people respond to decisions they did not make, how concerns are raised during discussion, how information moves through an organization, and how individuals contribute when they are not the final authority.

Throughout this book, we have explored several core ideas: how assumptions influence interpretation, how communication shapes trust, how decisions require responsible support, and how leadership and followership often exist at the same time.

Many of the situations described in earlier chapters may already feel familiar.

In this chapter, we will revisit some of those types of scenarios and consider a few additional examples through the lens of effective followership.

The goal is not to introduce entirely new concepts, but to practice applying the principles explored throughout the book.

When viewed through this lens, situations that may initially feel frustrating or ambiguous often become clearer.

This chapter focuses not only on recognizing these dynamics intellectually, but also on practicing a shift—from emotional or reactionary responses to more objective and strategic ones.

By revisiting familiar scenarios and examining new ones, you have an opportunity to pause, observe the situation without judgment, and consider how a thoughtful response might move the work forward—even when the stakes feel high.

Effective followership often begins in that moment: when individuals choose deliberate participation over immediate reaction.

What Happens in Reality

Scenario 1: A Decision You Disagree With

A leadership team meets to discuss a significant operational change.

Several options are presented, and members of the team share different perspectives about the potential direction.

After hearing the discussion, the senior leader responsible for the final decision selects a path that some members of the team do not believe is the strongest option.

In the days that follow, different responses begin to emerge.

Some leaders continue to express disagreement in conversations with their teams. They emphasize that the decision was made above them or that they had recommended a different approach.

Others take a different approach.

While they may still have concerns, they shift their attention toward helping their teams move forward. They focus on clarifying the reasoning behind the decision, identifying potential challenges, and supporting implementation.

The situation itself is not unusual.

The difference lies in how individuals choose to interpret and respond to the situation.

One response centers on distancing from the decision.
The other centers on participating in making the decision successful.

Effective followership does not require agreement with every decision. It requires contributing perspective during discussion, and once direction is set, supporting the work in a way that strengthens the leadership system.

Scenario 2: Limited Access to Information

A group of employees learns that a major decision has been made by senior leadership with limited consultation.

Some immediately assume that leaders intentionally withheld information or failed to consider other perspectives.

Others take a different approach.

They recognize that decision-making authority often involves balancing confidential information, time constraints, or strategic considerations that may not be visible to everyone in the organization.

Rather than assuming hidden motives, they seek additional context.

They ask thoughtful questions and attempt to understand the reasoning behind the decision.

This approach reflects an important principle explored earlier in this book:

Information you do not have is not always information that has been hidden.

Curiosity often leads to better understanding than assumption.

Scenario 3: Interpreting Leadership Silence

A team raises a concern about a developing issue and brings it to their leader for review.

After hearing the concern, the leader thanks the group for bringing it forward and says they will take time to consider the information before making a decision.

Several days pass without further communication.

During that time, different interpretations begin to circulate within the team.

Some employees assume the leader is ignoring the issue.

Others interpret the silence as a sign that the concern was not taken seriously.

A few begin speculating about hidden motives or internal politics that may be influencing the decision.

In reality, the leader is reviewing additional information, consulting with other departments, and considering several possible responses before determining the best course of action.

Situations like this are common in organizations.

When information is incomplete, people often fill the gaps with assumptions.

Effective followership requires a different approach.

Rather than immediately interpreting silence as dismissal or avoidance, strong followers remain curious about what might be happening behind the scenes.

They seek clarification when appropriate and recognize that decision-making often involves factors that are not immediately visible.

Maintaining curiosity in moments of uncertainty helps prevent misunderstandings from becoming unnecessary conflict.

Scenario 4: Raising a Concern

During a team discussion about a new initiative, one team member notices a potential challenge that could affect another department.

There are two ways this moment could unfold.

One option is silence during the meeting, followed by private conversations afterward expressing frustration about the proposal.

Another option is raising the concern directly during the discussion:

"I may be missing something, but I see a potential impact on this group that we may want to consider."

This allows the issue to be explored while the conversation is still focused on solving the problem.

Direct communication helps prevent concerns from becoming frustration later.

Effective followership requires the willingness to raise concerns constructively in the moment rather than expressing them indirectly after decisions are made.

Scenario 5: Joining a New Organization

A professional joins an organization with significant experience and a strong desire to contribute.

Within the first few weeks, they begin suggesting improvements to several existing processes based on practices they have seen elsewhere.

Members of the existing team respond by explaining that some processes are shaped by policies established by headquarters or by operational constraints that are not easily changed.

The new team member begins to feel that their ideas are being dismissed.

Meanwhile, the existing team may perceive the suggestions as criticism of systems they themselves do not control.

Effective followership requires understanding the system before attempting to reshape it.

Strong followers take time to learn how decisions are made, what constraints exist, and why certain practices developed the way they did.

Only then do they begin offering suggestions that are informed by context rather than assumption.

Experience is valuable.

Effective followership requires pairing it with curiosity.

Scenario 6: Protecting the Integrity of Information

In many organizations, information moves through multiple layers before reaching decision-makers.

A manager may summarize feedback from their team and communicate it upward.

A senior leader may interpret that information again when responding to the issue.

Over time, small shifts in how information is framed can create confusion or mistrust between levels of the organization.

Effective followership includes protecting the integrity of information.

Concerns shared upward should be represented accurately.
Decisions communicated downward should be explained clearly.

When information moves responsibly through an organization, trust is strengthened.

When it is filtered or distorted, misunderstandings quickly emerge.

Scenario 7: When Multiple Perspectives Collide

A leadership team meets to address a growing operational challenge that requires a significant change in how work is organized.

During the discussion, several perspectives emerge.

One leader raises concerns about how the change might affect their department's workload.
Another points out potential budget implications.
A third believes the proposal will ultimately strengthen the organization but acknowledges that it may create tension in the short term.

The senior leader responsible for the final decision listens to the discussion and ultimately chooses a path that addresses the long-term organizational need, even though several leaders expressed reservations.

In the days that follow, the team faces an important moment.

Some members of the group are tempted to continue debating the decision in private conversations. Others worry about how their teams will react and begin distancing themselves from the choice.

A different response is also possible.

Leaders can acknowledge that multiple perspectives raised during the discussion are valid. The concerns about workload, resources, and implementation may all be legitimate.

At the same time, they can recognize that the decision was made with the broader needs of the organization in mind.

Effective followership requires holding both realities at once.

Concerns may be valid.
Trade-offs may exist.
And the responsibility to help the organization move forward still remains.

In situations like this, strong followers shift their attention toward implementation. They help clarify the reasoning behind the decision, identify practical challenges that need to be addressed, and support their teams in adapting to the change.

Rather than revisiting the debate, they focus on strengthening the path forward.

Moments like this often reveal the difference between passive criticism and responsible followership.

Effective followers contribute their perspective during discussion, accept that leadership sometimes requires choosing among imperfect options, and help the organization move forward once direction has been established.

Reflection Prompt

Consider a recent situation in your organization where tension emerged around a decision, a communication breakdown, or differing perspectives about how work should move forward.

How did people respond in that moment?

Did individuals pause to understand the broader context, or did assumptions fill the gaps where information was incomplete?

Were concerns raised constructively during the discussion, or did they surface later in private conversations?

Once direction became clear, did people shift toward supporting the work—or distance themselves from responsibility for the outcome?

Looking back, which of the principles explored in this book were present in the situation?
Which were missing?

How might the outcome have been different if individuals involved had approached the moment with a more deliberate followership mindset?

Closing Reflection

The situations described in this chapter are not unusual.

They occur in organizations every day.

What distinguishes healthy leadership systems from dysfunctional ones is not the absence of disagreement, complexity, or difficult decisions.

It is how people respond in those moments.

Effective followership does not eliminate tension.

Instead, it helps ensure that tension moves ideas forward rather than pulling teams apart.

When individuals learn to pause, examine situations objectively, and respond with intention, they strengthen not only their own influence but also the functioning of the leadership systems around them.

Chapter 13

Discussion Prompts for Leaders & Teams

The Truth

The principles of effective followership are most powerful when they are discussed collectively.

Leadership rarely happens in isolation. Decisions are shaped by conversations, interpretation, and collaboration among people operating at different levels of authority.

For this reason, the ideas in this book are most useful when leadership teams examine them together.

The following prompts are designed to help teams reflect on how leadership and followership currently function within their organization—and how they might function more effectively.

These questions are not intended to produce immediate agreement.

Their purpose is to create space for honest conversation about how teams interpret information, raise concerns, support decisions, and share responsibility for organizational outcomes.

Discussion Prompt 1

How do we currently interpret incomplete information?

When decisions are made without full visibility across the organization, how do we typically respond?

Do we assume that information is being intentionally withheld, or do we begin with curiosity about what factors may not be visible to us?

What norms could help our team remain curious rather than reactionary when information is limited?

Discussion Prompt 2

How do we raise concerns within this team?

When someone sees a potential problem, what typically happens?

Do concerns surface during the conversation when decisions are being discussed, or do they tend to appear later in smaller conversations outside the room?

What would make it easier for people to raise concerns constructively in real time?

Discussion Prompt 3

How do we respond after a decision has been made?

Once a direction has been established, how does the team typically respond?

Do we consistently shift toward supporting implementation, or do we sometimes continue debating decisions in ways that create confusion for others?

What would responsible support look like in our context?

Discussion Prompt 4

How do we interpret disagreement?

When someone challenges an idea in this team, how is it usually interpreted?

Is disagreement seen as resistance, or as a contribution to improving the work?

What norms would help ensure that disagreement strengthens decisions rather than creating personal tension?

Discussion Prompt 5

How does information move through our organization?

When concerns move upward or decisions move downward, how confident are we that the message remains accurate?

Where do misunderstandings most often occur?

What practices could strengthen the integrity of communication across levels of the organization?

Discussion Prompt 6

When do we assume the best intent—and when do we assume the worst?

In moments of uncertainty, how often do we assume that others are acting thoughtfully but under constraints we may not see?

How often do we assume hidden motives or poor judgment?

How might our conversations change if we approached more situations with curiosity rather than suspicion?

Discussion Prompt 7

What does effective followership look like in this team?

If someone outside the organization observed our leadership team, what behaviors would signal strong followership?

Where are we already doing this well?

Where do we see opportunities to strengthen how we support each other's leadership?

Closing Reflection

Healthy leadership systems do not emerge from titles alone.

They emerge from the daily interactions between people who are willing to lead when needed, follow responsibly when appropriate, and share ownership for the success of the organization.

These conversations are one way to begin strengthening that system.

Chapter 14

The Effective Followership Agreement

The Truth

Organizations often invest significant time developing strategies, policies, and operational priorities.

Far less time is spent defining how people expect to participate in leadership together.

Yet the effectiveness of leadership teams depends not only on strategy, but also on how individuals communicate, challenge ideas, and support decisions.

The following agreement outlines a set of norms that leadership teams can adopt to strengthen the practice of effective followership within their organization.

These norms are not rules. They are shared commitments that help teams navigate difficult conversations, differing perspectives, and complex decisions with greater clarity and trust.

1. We Challenge Ideas Without Personalizing the Conversation

Disagreement is a normal and valuable part of responsible leadership.

Team members are encouraged to question assumptions, raise concerns, and offer alternative perspectives.

These conversations remain focused on improving ideas rather than criticizing individuals.

Our commitment:

We challenge ideas directly while maintaining respect for the people involved.

2. We Raise Concerns to Improve Decisions

Concerns are shared with the intention of strengthening the work—not simply documenting disagreement.

When someone raises an issue, the assumption is that they are contributing constructively to the decision-making process.

Our commitment:
We raise concerns early and clearly with the goal of improving decisions.

3. We Address Behavior Directly Rather Than Creating Broad Restrictions

Organizations sometimes respond to the actions of a small number of individuals by introducing policies that affect everyone.

Effective leadership systems address issues directly with the individuals involved whenever possible.

Our commitment:
We address concerns directly rather than creating unnecessary rules for the entire group.

4. We Create Shared Language for Difficult Conversations

Many professionals hesitate to raise important issues because they fear confrontation.

Teams can reduce this barrier by developing simple language models that allow concerns to be raised constructively.

Examples might include:

- "I want to pause and make sure we're addressing the underlying concern."

- "I may be misunderstanding something, but I see a potential risk here."

- "Can we explore another perspective before moving forward?"

Our commitment:
We use shared language that makes it easier to address difficult issues respectfully and early.

5. We Support Decisions Once They Are Made

Open discussion improves decision-making.

Once a decision has been made, the team shifts its focus toward implementation.

Supporting the decision does not require abandoning earlier perspectives. It requires recognizing the team's responsibility to move the work forward.

Our commitment:
We contribute honestly during discussion and support the work once direction is clear.

6. We Assume Responsibility for the System We Help Create

Every individual contributes to the culture of the team through their daily behavior.

Leadership systems are shaped not only by those with authority, but by how everyone participates.

Our commitment:

We recognize our role in strengthening the leadership system around us.

Final Reflection

In most organizations, leadership and followership are not separate identities.

They are responsibilities that people move between depending on the situation.

Strong organizations develop leaders.

Exceptional organizations develop people who understand how to lead and follow responsibly at the same time.

Effective followership makes that possible.

Chapter 15

Leading From Any Seat

Leading From Any Seat

Throughout this book, we have explored a concept that is often overlooked in discussions of leadership.

In most organizations, the majority of people operate without final decision authority. Yet the effectiveness of leadership systems depends not only on the decisions made at the top, but on how individuals throughout the organization interpret those decisions, communicate about them, and contribute to the work that follows.

Leadership and followership are often described as separate roles.
In practice, they are responsibilities that individuals move between every day.

A person may lead in one moment and follow in the next. They may hold authority in one context and operate without it in another.

The question, then, is not simply how to lead or how to follow.
The question is how to participate responsibly in the leadership system.

The Leadership Participation Model introduced in this book provides one way of understanding that responsibility.

It begins with awareness—recognizing that leadership is not confined to those with titles.
It requires interpretation—challenging assumptions about what is known, what is unknown, and how decisions are made.
It demands discipline—choosing to communicate clearly, raise concerns constructively, and support the work once direction is set.
And ultimately, it calls for integration—establishing shared norms that strengthen how leadership functions across teams.

These are not abstract ideas.

They are practiced in everyday moments.

When someone raises a concern directly rather than expressing it later in private.

When a team supports a decision they did not make and works to implement it effectively.

When information is communicated accurately rather than reshaped to serve individual preferences.

When individuals remain engaged in the work, even when the path forward is not the one they would have chosen.

In many organizations, frustration emerges not because leadership is absent, but because expectations for participation are unclear.

Leaders may expect initiative, while others expect direction.

Some individuals may interpret their role as supporting decisions quietly, while others believe they are expected to challenge and influence those decisions.

Without a shared understanding of how to participate, even well-intentioned teams can struggle.

The purpose of this book has not been to assign blame or to elevate one role over another.

It has been to clarify how leadership systems function—and how individuals contribute to those systems regardless of title.

Effective followership is not passive.

It is not compliance, nor is it quiet agreement.

It is the disciplined practice of leadership in moments when authority is not yours.

It requires judgment.
It requires clarity.
And it requires a willingness to participate in the work of leadership, even when doing so is uncomfortable.

The responsibility for effective leadership systems does not sit with a single individual.
It is shared.

It is shaped by how people communicate, how they interpret situations, and how they choose to engage with the work in front of them.

This is what it means to lead from any seat.

Not to hold authority, but to exercise responsibility.
Not to control decisions, but to contribute to how those decisions are understood and implemented.
Not to step back when authority is absent, but to step forward with intention.

In the end, leadership is not defined only by who makes the final decision.
It is defined by how people participate in the system that makes those decisions meaningful.

And in most organizations, that work happens every day—through individuals who understand how to lead from any seat.

Bring This Work Into Your Organization

If this framework resonates with you or your team, this work can be brought directly into your organization through:

- Leadership workshops

- Executive coaching

- Team development sessions

To learn more or inquire about bookings:

☞ **www.dsminitiatives.com**

References

Argyris, C. (1991). Teaching smart people how to learn. *Harvard Business Review, 69*(3), 99–109.

Bass, B. M., & Riggio, R. E. (2006). *Transformational leadership* (2nd ed.). Psychology Press.

Brown, B. (2018). *Dare to lead: Brave work. Tough conversations. Whole hearts.* Random House.

Carsten, M. K., Uhl-Bien, M., West, B. J., Patera, J. L., & McGregor, R. (2010). Exploring social constructions of followership: A qualitative study. *The Leadership Quarterly, 21*(3), 543–562. https://doi.org/10.1016/j.leaqua.2010.03.015

Collins, J. (2001). *Good to great: Why some companies make the leap… and others don't.* HarperBusiness.

Edmondson, A. C. (2019). *The fearless organization: Creating psychological safety in the workplace for learning, innovation, and growth.* Wiley.

Edmondson, A. C., & Lei, Z. (2014). Psychological safety: The history, renaissance, and future of an interpersonal construct. *Annual Review of Organizational Psychology and Organizational Behavior, 1*, 23–43. https://doi.org/10.1146/annurev-orgpsych-031413-091305

Graen, G. B., & Uhl-Bien, M. (1995). Relationship-based approach to leadership: Development of leader–member exchange (LMX) theory. *The Leadership Quarterly, 6*(2), 219–247. https://doi.org/10.1016/1048-9843(95)90036-5

Greenleaf, R. K. (1977). *Servant leadership: A journey into the nature of legitimate power and greatness.* Paulist Press.

Heifetz, R. A., Grashow, A., & Linsky, M. (2009). *The practice of adaptive leadership: Tools and tactics for changing your organization and the world.* Harvard Business Press.

Hollander, E. P. (1992). Leadership, followership, self, and others. *The Leadership Quarterly, 3*(1), 43–54. https://doi.org/10.1016/1048-9843(92)90003-O

Kellerman, B. (2007). What every leader needs to know about followers. *Harvard Business Review, 85*(12), 84–91.

Kellerman, B. (2008). *Followership: How followers are creating change and changing leaders.* Harvard Business Press.

Lencioni, P. (2002). *The five dysfunctions of a team: A leadership fable.* Jossey-Bass.

Northouse, P. G. (2022). *Leadership: Theory and practice* (9th ed.). Sage Publications.

Schein, E. H., & Schein, P. (2018). *Humble leadership: The power of relationships, openness, and trust.* Berrett-Koehler.

Uhl-Bien, M., Riggio, R. E., Lowe, K. B., & Carsten, M. K. (2014). Followership theory: A review and research agenda. *The Leadership Quarterly, 25*(1), 83–104. https://doi.org/10.1016/j.leaqua.2013.11.007

Uhl-Bien, M., & Ospina, S. M. (Eds.). (2012). *Advancing relational leadership research: A dialogue among perspectives.* Information Age Publishing.

Yukl, G. (2013). *Leadership in organizations* (8th ed.). Pearson.

Acknowledgements

This book was shaped by the many leadership experiences, conversations, and challenges that have influenced how I understand organizations and the people within them.

I am grateful to the colleagues, clients, and teams I have had the opportunity to work alongside. Your willingness to engage in honest conversations about leadership, trust, and organizational dynamics has informed much of the thinking reflected in these pages.

I also appreciate those who have challenged my perspectives over time. Those moments—while not always comfortable—played an important role in helping me refine how I approach leadership and followership.

To those who have supported me personally, thank you for your encouragement, patience, and understanding throughout this process.

This work is not the result of a single experience, but of many moments that have shaped how I understand leadership—and the responsibility we each carry within it.

About the Author

Sandra Miles, PhD is a leadership consultant, facilitator, and founder of DSM Initiatives, LLC, where she partners with organizations to strengthen leadership effectiveness, communication, and trust across teams.

With more than two decades of experience in leadership roles, Sandra brings a practitioner's perspective to complex organizational dynamics. Her work focuses on helping leaders and teams navigate change, align around shared goals, and build cultures grounded in accountability and clarity.

Through executive coaching, leadership development, and facilitated sessions, she supports organizations in developing leadership systems that extend beyond formal authority.

Sandra is also the founder of Lumithéa, a beauty brand rooted in the belief that self-care is a form of leadership. Her work across both organizations reflects a consistent focus on intentionality, presence, and the connection between how individuals show up and how systems function.

Leading From Any Seat reflects her commitment to helping individuals and organizations better understand how leadership operates at every level.

For speaking and consulting inquiries, visit www.dsminitiatives.com